STUDY GUIDE

THIS
INVITATIONAL
LIFE

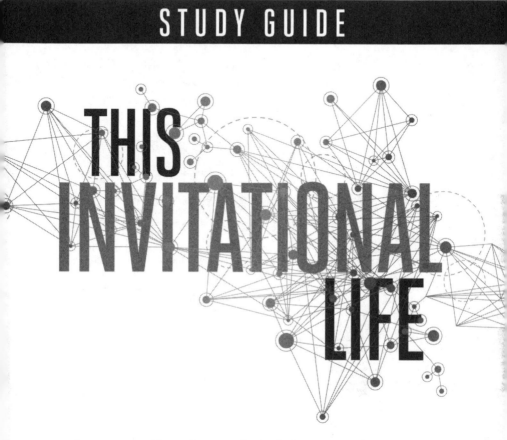

THIS INVITATIONAL LIFE

risking *yourself* to align with God's heartbeat for humanity

STEVE CARTER

David C Cook®
transforming lives together

THIS INVITATIONAL LIFE STUDY GUIDE
Published by David C Cook
4050 Lee Vance View
Colorado Springs, CO 80918 U.S.A.

David C Cook U.K., Kingsway Communications
Eastbourne, East Sussex BN23 6NT, England

The graphic circle C logo is a registered trademark of David C Cook.

ISBN 978-0-7814-1399-2
eISBN 978-1-4347-1103-8

© 2016 Stephen Carter

The Team: Alice Crider, Stephen and Amanda Sorenson, Nick
Lee, Kathy Mosier, Helen Macdonald, Susan Murdock
Cover Design: Amy Konyndyk
Cover Photo: iStockphoto

Printed in the United States of America
First Edition 2016

1 2 3 4 5 6 7 8 9 10

052716

CONTENTS

PREFACE

God loves to work with his people in order to bring about good in the world he created. And for those of us who have accepted God's gift of redemption, every moment of life is brimming with redemptive potential. We never know ahead of time when opportunities for redemption will arise or what they will look like, but God makes his invitation clear. How we respond is up to us.

That's why Ananias is my hero. He was an ordinary, everyday Christ follower who is mentioned in only a few verses of the Bible (see Acts 9:10–19). He loved his city and his church and wanted to maximize the moments of life for the good of God's kingdom. So when God called to him, he responded with a simple "Yes, Lord." When God invited him to participate in a high-stakes task in God's work of redemption, he did it!

That's what is so amazing to me. God invited Ananias to go to a specific house in Damascus to pray with Saul of Tarsus. Praying with someone may not seem to us like a big redemptive commitment, but at that time Saul was a violent man dead set on crushing the movement of Christ by destroying as many of his followers as possible (see vv. 1–9)!

I've often wondered, *What if Ananias had said no?* What if, when God asked him to go to Saul, he had given in to self-doubt and fear and had opted out? The New Testament story would certainly be very different, and Ananias would have missed out on the full, rich life of faith God offers to those he redeems.

Responding to God's urging with a courageous yes leads us into a deeper and more trusting relationship with him. But so often we miss out on God's invitation to join him in his redemptive work. We make excuses by declaring that we're not qualified. We doubt our authority or ability to discern his voice. We're afraid of being misunderstood or rejected, uncomfortable or overzealous. For a slew of reasons we justify saying no to God's invitation.

Every time a Jesus follower says no to God's invitation, the church suffers. Individual people suffer, families suffer, and communities and cities suffer. Why? Because Christians are the means by which God intends to bring his love to every inch of this hurting world. For God's goodness to grow and expand, for that which is broken to be restored, and for hope to be rekindled, we have to participate in the opportunities God offers. We have to take the bold step and say yes to this invitational life.

The God of all heaven and earth invites us to align ourselves with his heartbeat for humanity. We can do this! We can learn to live deeply with Jesus, show up with expectation, relate well with everyone, and risk it all for what matters most to God.

I challenge you to consider the possibility that God is calling your name—that he is inviting you to act on behalf of his kingdom. How will you reply?

Two simple words, "Yes, Lord," will expose you to countless opportunities to partner with God in transforming the life story of a person, a family, a school, a city, or even a nation for God's kingdom. Are you in? Will you say yes to this invitational life?

Steve Carter
April 2016

PART I
LIVE

The invitational life isn't just about finding ways to invite someone into your faith; it's also about discovering how you can be invited into the lives of those around you.

SESSION 1
GOD'S STORY, OUR STORY

God's story is my story is your story is every person's story. Aligning ourselves with God's heartbeat for humanity means diving into all of it.

CONSIDER THE INVITATION

(4 minutes)

There are times when we can't escape the haunting questions of life. It may be when we face illness, relational struggles, or vocational setbacks. It may be when we lose someone who has significantly influenced our identity, our spiritual walk, or our sense of purpose or accomplishment. No matter what the catalyst, we at times find ourselves wondering what impact our life has on the world around us and what we represent to the people we encounter every day. We question whether our life—our story—has value and meaning that point to God and his love for all of humanity.

How important do you think it is for each of us to believe that our life has meaning and significance?

What are some of the things we pursue in our efforts to live a significant life, and where do they lead?

What are some of the distractions or obstacles that seem to prevent us from experiencing a truly significant life?

LET'S PRAY TOGETHER

Dear Lord, we come to you today thankful for who you are and for your presence with us as we begin this study. We ask that through our experience today you will draw us deeper into relationship with you, your community, and your redemptive work in this world. Please open our hearts and minds to what you desire us to learn and apply in our everyday lives so that our lives will make a difference and others will be drawn into a personal relationship with you. We want to align ourselves with your heartbeat for all of humanity, to discover more about living the love and truth of Jesus among those we meet, especially those who are different from us and may not even believe that you exist. Guide us during the coming weeks as we explore our walk of faith and how living this invitational life draws people to you. In the name of Jesus we pray, amen.

VIDEO HIGHLIGHTS

(15 minutes)

God's story

Our story

VIDEO CONVERSATION

(6 minutes)

1. As you watched the video, what did you discover about the relationship between every person's life story—including your life story—and God's story?

How might this new perspective alter your thinking about your life story, the way you live out your faith, or how you view other people?

2. How do you see God's great story of redemption making sense of the struggle, or fall, that plays out in your life story?

3. What did you realize about living this invitational life from the way Dominic and Nathan became part of Steve's life and invited him to become part of theirs?

BIBLE INVESTIGATION

(15 minutes)

When we consider the story of our life—who we are and why we exist—we quickly realize that many voices have spoken into our story and not all of what we have heard is good or true. Our family environment, for example, helps define how we see ourselves and our place in the world. Our family experience may build us up to approach life with confidence, security, and competence, or it may break us down so that we face the world feeling abandoned, fearful, and ashamed. Our peers, teachers, employers, political leaders, entertainers, and many other voices clamor to define who we are (or ought to be), assess our value, and prescribe our reasons to exist. Sadly, all this input can make it difficult for us to find our way in our own life story.

Fortunately, the voice of God, Creator of the universe, calls out above the voices of this world. He proclaims a different story, and it is amazing. As we explore God's big story in the Bible, we learn that

God's story includes us and that our story is part of his unfolding story! So let's take a look at the five great movements of God's story and see what they reveal about who we are and our role within his story.

1. God's story began with creation.

After creating light, sky, seas, land, plants, and animals, what did God create and why? (See Gen. 1:1–28.)

What was unique about God's creation of the human race, the capstone of his creation? (See 2:7, 18–23.)

In what ways does the Bible's description of the way God created human beings help us better understand the nature of our identity, value, and relationship with him?

2. God's story suffered the fall, a breakdown of relationship.

What did the serpent—representing evil, hate, deceit—accomplish, and what impact did his actions have on the harmony and trust that Adam and Eve experienced with God in the garden of Eden? (See 3:1–8.)

What did God do to invite Adam and Eve back into relationship after they separated themselves and hid from him? (See 3:9.)

What chaos resulted in creation and in the relationship between God and Adam and Eve? (See 3:14–24.)

3. God's story endured frustration and struggle.

After Adam and Eve's breach of trust with their creator, what domino effect occurred as people lived apart from an intimate relationship with God? (See 4:1–14; 6:5–8.)

In what ways did God's people, and even the leaders he chose to teach and guide them so they would represent him to the people of the world, struggle to live in relationship with him? (See Exod. 32:7–8; Judg. 21:25; 1 Sam. 8:1–9; Ps. 81:11–12.)

Since the fall, we all face a similar struggle in our relationship with God. In fact, we're a mess. What invitation and hope does God hold out to us in the midst of our struggle? (See Isa. 55:6–11.)

4. God's story provides redemption.

From the beginning God planned to redeem his fallen creation. What powerful and holy work did Jesus come to this broken, sin-filled earth to accomplish? (See Mark 10:45; John 1:29; 3:16; Eph. 1:7–10; Col. 1:13–14, 21–22.)

Jesus's life and work on earth displayed for us God's commitment to righteousness, justice, and reconciliation. What did obedience to God require of him and provide for us? (See Rom. 3:21–26.)

5. God's story invites us to join in the work of restoration.

God invites everyone who accepts his gift of redemption to partici-
pate with him in making this world everything he intended it to be.
How does the Bible describe what God's restoration looks like? (See
Isa. 11:6–9; 65:17–19; Rom. 8:19–21.)

What are those of us who have received Jesus as Lord and Savior
called to *be* and *do* in relation to God's story of redemption and
restoration? (See 2 Cor. 5:14–20.)

OUR LIFE RESPONSE

(4 minutes)

Each one of us has a story that begins with being a uniquely created
and beloved child of the living God. We were created for relationship

with God and others, and we have a unique role in God's story as it unfolds. Where do you see yourself in God's story?

For a long time I (Steve) didn't see myself as having a story, much less a story intertwined with God's great story. When my father left home for good, I experienced a fall that brought on a seemingly insurmountable struggle with identity, immense shame, and a deep striving to earn personal worth and the love of others. Fortunately, as I shared in the video, two guys found me when I was in junior high and demonstrated God's grace and love for me.

They lived the invitational life, and it made all the difference. They spent time with me, learning who I was and what motivated me. They became involved with me and poured into my life, in effect jumping into the water to save me as I was drowning.

They invited me to take the first simple step to live my life with Jesus, and God began healing my broken, fearful, and ashamed heart. They stuck with me as I accepted the invitation to go deeper with Jesus and wrestle with my doubts, emotions, and pressing questions. I continued discovering how to press into God when my faith was challenged and discovered that God is good. His invitation to receive redemption and restoration is true and trustworthy. Because of it, I can join in God's story and be a light in the darkness. By his grace I can live this invitational life—and you can too.

In what ways do you see God shaping your story today?

What has been your area(s) of struggle—the fall—that has separated you from living life in the kind of relationship God created you to have with him and others?

How is he meeting you in your struggle, healing you, and making you new again?

Who has come alongside you to earn your trust, talk with you, invite you to discover Jesus as your Savior, and demonstrate this invitational life?

How might God be nudging you to take the risk of being known by others by entering into the pain of another person's story and sharing the news of God's redemption and restoration?

Are you willing to share with others your story of how God met you in your struggle—perhaps feelings of abandonment or pain, a struggle with addiction, an insatiable drive to succeed—and made sense of it all by redeeming and restoring you?

TAKE ACTION

As you live your life this week, ask God to show you specific people to pray for—people who need an invitation to life with Jesus. Write down their names, keep their faces in mind, and pray boldly for them daily.

Ask God to show you places where he wants you to put this invitational life on display. Write them down.

Look, listen, and prepare for opportunities unique to those places that give you an entrée to display this invitational life.

Pray boldly not only for opportunities but also for the people who need Jesus and for your faithfulness in living out this invitational life, no matter how great the cost.

BENEDICTION

(1 minute)

May God, who has made us good by the atoning blood of Jesus, give us his grace to live this invitational life. May we trust in his sufficiency and boldly pursue the good work of inviting others to join in his story.

SESSION 2
CARRIERS OR BARRIERS?

When we say yes to this invitational way of living, we're saying yes to a front-row seat to seeing lives absolutely restored as they are brought into relationship with God.

CONSIDER THE INVITATION

(4 minutes)

As we closed our session together last time, we turned our attention to our daily lives and the people and places where this invitational life—our life story—can make a difference in inviting people to experience a restored relationship with God.

Which places can you put this invitational life on display?

What might you need to be more conscious of or do differently in order to be a better carrier of God's grace to people in those environments?

As you consider the people you identified (you don't need to share their names), which ones might need an invitation to living life with Jesus? What might be your first steps to show you care about their life stories and to open up your life story to them?

LET'S PRAY TOGETHER

Dear Lord, we thank you for giving us the privilege to live lives of profound significance that bring the saving grace of your kingdom to this earth. Thank you for breathing your life into us and entrusting your story of redemption to us so that we can live it and share it. As we delve into learning how to live this invitational life, we ask that you will guide and bless us so that others will come to know you and by your grace root their life story in your story. Be with us now as we explore the barriers we erect that prevent us from being effective carriers of your powerful, life-changing story. In Jesus's name we pray, amen.

VIDEO HIGHLIGHTS

(15 minutes)

The invitational life draws people in.

The cross is a barrier breaker.

VIDEO CONVERSATION

(6 minutes)

1. What did you think about as you imagined the scene of the service for Hal, Steve's mentor?

In what ways did that service indicate that Hal's life story mattered, that he had lived an invitational life?

2. What would you say are some of the characteristics of a life that invites people in, a life that showcases the cross of Jesus as a barrier breaker?

3. Sometimes we knowingly make isolating choices or judgments that can be barriers to people discovering the true character of God. What are some examples of these?

4. Even when we don't want to put up barriers that turn people away from experiencing God's grace, we sometimes do. What things might we feel, think, do, or say that unintentionally create barriers for people who have not yet discovered who the God of the Bible is?

BIBLE INVESTIGATION

(15 minutes)

We don't have to look far to realize that we live in a very broken world among people who desperately need a restored relationship with their creator. Differences and barriers between people are evident everywhere—conflicts between nations, within communities, and even among family members. These barriers are nothing new. The human race has been building relational barriers since the fall in the garden of Eden when sin first entered the world. Early in Genesis we see that people established social barriers and then constructed physical barriers, using stone and bricks to build cities and walls to protect themselves from "other" people outside their community. During the time Jesus lived on earth, the barrier between Jews and Gentiles, righteous and unrighteous could not have been stronger.

But the redemptive power of the cross of Jesus changes everything! The redemption of the cross obliterates all dividing walls. It replaces hostility with peace. The cross makes all who believe into an entirely new race of people who embody what the cross looks like in flesh and sweat and blood. For what reason? So that we—and all of humanity—can be invited to have full access to the Father. Let's see what we can learn from the early believers about how to become carriers of the gospel of Christ who invite people to know God rather than being barriers who keep people away from God.

1. What did Paul write in Ephesians 2:11–16 to address the divide that existed between Jews and Gentiles in the world *and* in the growing church of Jesus at the time?

What significance does this teaching have on how followers of Jesus today seek to live in a way that draws in all types of people and welcomes them to God's table?

In what ways does this passage address our tendency in the body of Christ to hold on to our differences and former barriers and thereby destroy the peace Jesus brought about through his suffering, death, and resurrection?

2. In contrast to holding on to our former ways, what impact do you think a lifestyle of inclusiveness and mutual support of one another has on displaying God's story of redemption and peace to people who do not yet know him? (See vv. 19–22.)

3. Learning to live the invitational life—a life that carries the message of reconciliation and peace through the cross of Jesus—required a major change of perspective for the early believers who were steeped in the Jew/Gentile divide. What powerful public statement did Peter make when he entered the house of a Gentile, probably for the first time in his life? (See Acts 10:27–29.)

4. It is not an exaggeration to say that it took an act of God for the early followers of Jesus to realize the power of the cross in breaking down the barriers that kept people from discovering what God did to redeem and restore us to relationship with him. Read Acts 21:26–32, and discuss the uproar that occurred when Jews thought Paul had brought Gentiles into the temple of God.

Living the invitational life—being a true carrier of God's grace to people who are on the "outside"—may be costly, as it nearly was for Paul. Our efforts may be misunderstood or misjudged. What might that cost look like in our communities and among our friends, families, and fellow believers?

5. God has always wanted his people—whether the patriarchs and Israelites of the Old Testament, the faithful Jews of Jesus's day, or the community of Jesus followers today—to participate in his unfolding story of redemption. He has called his people to make him known to "outsiders" and invite them into his story of redemption and restoration. What do Isaiah 42:5–7 and Micah 6:8 teach us about the kind of redemptive lives God wants his people to live before others?

6. When we follow Jesus, we take with us a message of redemption and reconciliation with God that breaks down barriers and brings peace not only in our relationship with God but also in our relationships with other people, particularly our fellow believers. As we engage together to live and share God's redemptive story, what do

we learn about how God wants us to treat one another? (See Rom. 12:18; 14:1, 19; 15:7; Heb. 12:14.)

OUR LIFE RESPONSE

(4 minutes)

Not everyone was given access to worship God at Herod's temple in Jerusalem. There was a hierarchy of who was allowed in and who was kept out. Gentiles could not pass the balustrade into the inner courts. Women were allowed into their court inside the temple gates but not into the court of Israel where men could worship. Even priests were allowed to enter the holy temple only at designated times.

Jesus sacrificed his life on the cross so that all of humanity— every single person, no matter how good or bad, unimpressive or great—could receive forgiveness and cleansing from sin and have access to the Father. Think about it. One meaning of the word *access* in Greek is "to have an audience with the king." Jesus came to earth so that all people—people like us and people who are quite different from us—could experience a personal relationship with the King!

We are supposed to be like God's temple, the place where people can experience what God is like. How accurately does your life represent what Jesus is like and what he did on the cross?

When it comes to inviting people who do not know God to his table, are you a carrier or a barrier?

What in your life invites people to discover what God has done for you? What pushes them away from relationship with you or God?

To what extent does your life welcome people from diverse backgrounds to experience God's grace? Are you more inclined to neglect, ignore, fear, or judge people who aren't like you?

TAKE ACTION

Jesus demonstrated by his life that each and every person who walks this earth is just one prayer away from joining God's story. Every follower of Jesus has a part in inviting people into God's story.

Who in your life is God leading you to pray for so that he or she may discover Jesus and become a participant in God's story?

What commitment will you make today to pray for that person?

Not one of us will live this invitational life perfectly. There will be times when we allow circumstances to overwhelm us, when we stumble in our walk with God, and when we, for a time or in a particular situation, become barriers to God's story rather than carriers. But our shortcomings don't change the story. God's plan of redemption is advancing. By the power of the cross, our identity is that of barrier breakers who carry the story and peace of God into our desperately needy world.

Which specific barriers in your life and relationships with others do you need to address?

What are you willing to do in order to break down each of those barriers and offer a seat at the table to those who need to join God's story?

BENEDICTION

(1 minute)

Be filled with joy! We have the privilege of being carriers of the peace of Christ to a broken world that does not know him. May his peace rule in our hearts as we live in a way that invites all God's beloved children to be restored to the Father.

PART II
SHOW UP

This invitational life is all about sharing with those you meet the good news that there is a God who loves them, pursues them, and believes in them.

SESSION 3
SHOWING UP FOR EVERYONE

As God's adopted children, we have received his heritage of acceptance and love. So we must devote ourselves to living as he does, wholeheartedly and unabashedly searching for ways to extend unconditional love to others.

CONSIDER THE INVITATION

(4 minutes)

As we closed our previous session together, we turned our attention to how we live out our identity in Christ by being *carriers* of God's story rather than *barriers* to people who need to be invited into his story.

As you prayed for the specific person who is just one prayer away from joining God's story, what did God's Spirit reveal to you about how you can be a carrier of his redemptive grace to him or her?

Did God show you barriers that need to be addressed in your relationship with that person? If so, how do you believe he wants you to deal with them? What are you doing to break down those barriers?

When we desire to live the invitational life, it's not easy to face the barriers we have created in our relationships with others. But what vision and hope does God give us for what he can accomplish in a person's life if we are willing to break down those barriers?

In what ways does recognizing our identity as barrier breakers and living accordingly set us free to wholeheartedly show up for people who need an invitation into God's story?

LET'S PRAY TOGETHER

Dear Lord, we thank you for choosing us as your own and giving us the privilege of participating in your great story of love and grace, redemption and restoration. Guided by your Spirit within us, may we seek to know your heart and fully share your desire to extend your love and invitation to redemption to everyone we encounter. Be with us now as we delve deeper into your story to discover how to live a life that is fully engaged with your redemptive purpose. May we learn to show up for all people, no matter what their background or persuasion may be. In the precious name of Jesus we pray, amen.

VIDEO HIGHLIGHTS

(15 minutes)

We are not alone: God's Spirit is working within us.

We are not powerless: God's Spirit is at work in the world around us.

VIDEO CONVERSATION

(6 minutes)

1. Since before time began, the Spirit has been at work, step by step, with God the Father. What does the paradigm shift that took place at Pentecost mean to you? What difference does it make to you that God's Spirit descended on and empowered *every* believer to fulfill God's work and that the Spirit's presence is no longer given only to kings, priests, prophets, and others who have been set apart for a special role in God's story?

2. In the ancient city of Ephesus, where anyone could pick up unwanted, discarded infants and raise them as slaves, *adoption* that granted a person status as a son or daughter made a powerful statement. How do you imagine the Ephesian believers responded when

they realized that God had adopted them as his own beloved children—choosing them and giving them a new, perfect, and blameless identity?

How do you think their adoption into God's family and story inspired them to live the invitational life and share that good news with everyone they knew?

What impact does God's adoption of us—the fact that he has lavished his love on us and given us a new, holy, and blameless identity—have on our desire to faithfully extend his unconditional love to those who do not yet know him?

3. God's Spirit is at work not only within those of us who have been redeemed by God's grace. The Spirit is at work in the whole world, seeking to reconcile all of creation to God. In what ways do you think the Spirit's work in the world ought to influence our day-to-day lives?

To what extent do we approach the invitational life with an attitude of great expectancy and an eager awareness that God is at work, which then prompts us to look for opportunities in which he wants us to join in?

What can happen when we actively listen to the voice of God's Spirit? What results when we put the Spirit's promptings on mute?

BIBLE INVESTIGATION

(15 minutes)

God's boundless love compels him to show up for us—to seek, save, and restore us. He chooses us in love, adopting us into his family just as we are. By the redeeming power of the cross, he forgives and cancels our impossible debt of sin. By his grace, he creates for each of us a new identity as his beloved child and gives us a second chance at life. Even more amazing, he invites us to show up for others who are just as needy, vulnerable, and desperate as we once were. Let's consider what the Bible shows us about how important it is for us to show up and invite all people into God's great story of redemption.

1. In contrast to the dominant Hellenistic culture of Ephesus that rejected, discarded, and abandoned anyone who lacked physical perfection or didn't measure up or fit in, what does God declare to be true about the value of each and every person? (See Eph. 1:3–10.)

Why should it matter to us as Jesus followers in our world today, as it did to Jesus followers in ancient Ephesus, that God, our creator, is a God of love who highly values, chooses, pursues, and even adopts into his family everyone who accepts his gift of redemption?

What are we left with if we do not have our God?

2. Even though everyone around us may overlook us, ignore us, and consider us to be unimportant, insignificant, or invisible, who shows up for us? (See Ps. 139:1–16.)

What does it mean for us that God is actively watchful and aware of our every thought and action?

What can we learn about God's loving awareness and care for us, and how can we apply it as we seek to live the invitational life and show up for others?

3. Why is the cross such powerful proof that the one true God shows up for us and doesn't abandon us to face the forces of evil on our own? (See Gal. 4:4–7.)

4. In Romans 10:13 what did Paul remind the church in Rome about whom God is willing to save, and why is this important for us to remember?

In what ways might this expansive view of extending God's invitation to *everyone* be a bit threatening to us? Be a relief to us?

5. During the time Jesus lived on earth, the only area of the temple in Jerusalem where Gentiles were permitted to enter had become a hub of commercial activity. How did Jesus respond to the fact that Gentiles, people who desperately needed to encounter God, were hindered from worshipping there? (See Matt. 21:12–13.)

How does what we have learned about God's desire for all people to be welcome at his table and to be invited into a redemptive relationship with him help you understand the intensity of Jesus's response to the situation?

OUR LIFE RESPONSE

(4 minutes)

In every environment and place, God's Spirit is at work so that people who need God may come to know him. Read Jesus's story in Luke 14:16–23 about whom God invites to his banquet, whom he invites to accept his gift of redemption and join his family.

How important is it to God that everyone receives his invitation?

To what extent do you share God's desire to invite everyone to his table, and how does that desire affect your daily life?

Each of us who has been redeemed by the blood of Jesus is a carrier of God's grace, a servant who invites people to the Master's banquet. When our Master says, "Go, invite everyone," how do we respond?

Is your definition of "everyone" the same as God's, or are there some you would rather not show up for? If so, what changes in life and attitude might you make in order to align your definition more closely with God's?

In Jesus's story the master urged his servants to hurry and search everywhere for everyone who had not yet been invited. To what extent do you share God's urgency to fill his table to overflowing?

TAKE ACTION

God welcomes everyone to his table. He has called those he has adopted as his very own to show up and invite others—no matter who they are—to a place at God's table. We see an example of this when Paul and Barnabas went to Pisidian Antioch. They showed up and took the opportunity that the Spirit presented to share God's story in the local synagogue. The people invited them back the next week, and nearly the whole city came to hear them (see Acts 13)!

What are you anticipating God will do when you invite everyone to his table?

What does your commitment to be an active participant in fulfilling God's great story of redemption require of you?

Who will you show up for this week? Where do you have to go and what do you have to do in order to seek out that person?

What specific things will you pray for in regard to living out the invitational life with that person in mind?

Why is it important to listen carefully to the promptings of God's Spirit as you look for the opportunities God has prepared for you to extend his invitation to that person?

What will you do to set aside the everyday distractions and keep yourself tuned in to God's voice and the Spirit's guidance in living the invitational life?

BENEDICTION

(1 minute)

May God, who has established us as his children, holy and blameless in his sight, cause us to be so filled with love for all people that we will be faithful servants who engage in every good work that invites people into God's family.

SESSION 4
SCATTERING SEEDS OF GRACE

Looking for good in another person is like digging for gold.
We look for good within a culture that is so cynical, angry,
and judgmental that random acts of kindness are seen as
extraordinary. By looking for good and pointing people to
what is truly good, we become a compelling force of grace.

CONSIDER THE INVITATION

(4 minutes)

As we closed our session together last time, we turned our attention
to intentionally showing up and, prompted by God's Spirit, doing
our part to invite everyone to God's table.

Who did you show up for? (You don't need to share the person's name.) What did you expect God to do, and what happened?

In what ways were you aware of God's preparation of your heart and actions, the opportunity he provided, and the person you were led to show up for?

In what ways did your recognition of God's presence in the process empower you to extend his invitation to that person or to begin building a sincere relationship?

From what you have experienced so far, what opportunities are you expecting God to put before you to scatter seeds of grace that lead to redemption and restoration for everyone who needs to know God?

LET'S PRAY TOGETHER

Dear Lord, we live in a world where people so often grasp the best for themselves and offer nothing but criticism, rejection, and abandonment to those they feel don't measure up. Yet you, Lord, show up with reckless love and joyfully redeem, restore, and embrace everyone who calls on your name. Thank you, Lord. You are our Savior. We are blessed and privileged to be called your children. We gratefully accept your calling to live a life that invites others into your story to experience a relationship of redemption and hope with you. Teach us to live in a way that spreads your boundless grace far and wide. In Jesus's name we pray, amen.

VIDEO HIGHLIGHTS

(15 minutes)

Look for the good; look for the need.

Massevot—what happened here?

VIDEO CONVERSATION

(6 minutes)

1. It is appropriate for us to take seriously the responsibility and opportunities we have to share the message of God's grace with everyone. But we sometimes approach the privilege in a dutiful, judgmental, and impersonal manner that lacks the vibrant life, joy, and love that restoration to God's story brings. As you imagined a little boy gleefully throwing fistfuls of birdseed into the air, what effect did that image have on how you want to live your life for God?

How much do you want your life with God to be significant and filled with expectation, vitality, joy, and hope?

What impact do you think such a life will have on those whose story doesn't yet have a vital connection with God's story?

2. In what ways is the life and character of a person who looks for the good in others a powerful testimony of grace? If you have ever known such a person, what impact did he or she have on you?

What do you think looking for and recognizing the good in another person does for building a connection and relationship with him or her?

Why is looking for the good in other people an important characteristic of the invitational life?

3. When have you encountered a person whose life was so full, win-
some, and intriguing that it demanded an explanation?

What was the reason behind that person's unique life, and what did
you learn from him or her about living life well?

4. What do you think God desires people to see in our lives—in our
character, our priorities, our conversations, our actions—that is so
powerful they want to know more about us and are compelled to ask,
"What is happening?"

BIBLE INVESTIGATION

(15 minutes)

As followers of Jesus, we have a high calling to pursue. Once we have called on the name of the Lord and been redeemed, God gives us a job to do. Having become our redeemer, rescuer, and Savior, he sends us out to share our story with everyone who will listen. Through the example of our lives and words, we are to scatter the good news of what it is like to experience God's goodness. So let's take a closer look at how we can go about living the invitational life in ways that extend God's grace to everyone.

1. Read carefully what Paul explained in Romans 10:14 about how those who do not yet know or believe in God can come to know him. What is the process of knowing and believing in God?

What responsibility does every one of us who has experienced God's redemption have in this life-changing process?

2. Who does God send out to bring the good news so that every person will have the opportunity to call on the name of the Lord? (See Rom. 10:15; Eph. 2:4–10; 1 Pet. 4:10–11.)

In what ways and by whom have God's redeemed people been equipped to accomplish this mission?

Who sustains God's people and provides the strength needed to share the good news?

What does God's Word say about those who bring the good news to everyone who needs to hear it, and what encouragement does this truth provide for the task?

3. God's great story of redemption and restoration of all who are separated from him by sin is punctuated with great acts that invite us to look closer and discover what he is doing. God's people often have celebrated or memorialized occasions when he acted mightily in their lives so that future generations would see and remember what happened and glorify God. Let's consider a few of these instances and note how the work of God was recognized and remembered.

Passage	What happened	How it was remembered
Genesis 32:24–30	Jacob wrestled with God and lived.	
Exodus 14:26–31; 15:1–18	The Israelites crossed the Red Sea safely; the Egyptians did not.	
Exodus 24:1–5	Israel made a commitment to obey everything the Lord commanded.	
Joshua 3:14–17; 4:1–9, 19–24	God stopped the waters of the Jordan River so the Israelites could cross on dry ground.	

4. It is important not only for God's people to remember and glorify him for what he has done, but also for people who do not know God need to see such memorials—*massevot* in Hebrew—so that they ask the question, "What happened here?" What kind of a memorial did Peter say God intends followers of Jesus to be? (See 1 Pet. 2:4–5, 9.)

In what sense do we become "living stones" as we live the invitational life?

OUR LIFE RESPONSE

(4 minutes)

For those of us who follow Jesus, there is no greater joy, honor, or fulfillment than to participate in another person's story as he or she discovers God's story and chooses to join in.

How do we get to that point? How do we develop lives that demand an explanation that leads other people to God?

We begin by living intentionally. Peter wrote, "Always be prepared to give an answer to everyone who asks you to give the reason for the hope that you have" (1 Pet. 3:15). We prepare by going deep with Jesus, by reading God's Word daily, by asking God to teach us something new about him and his calling for us, by seeking to be more aware of his presence, and by following his leading.

How are you preparing to live the invitational life?

If you have neglected this area of your life, what are you willing to commit to in order to be prepared to give an answer for your hope?

We show up with great expectancy for what God will do. God's redeeming presence is everywhere. He is always there for his children. He never fails us. When we go where he asks us to go, he will always meet us there. He will open doors, prepare hearts, and give us the right words to speak.

Expectancy is the birthplace of dependency on God, who always desires our partnership in what he is doing. To what extent do you trust God to provide for you when you take a risk, when you go where he asks you to go?

We spark ongoing relationships. We spend time in the places and with the people we have prayed over so that we can build relationships that last and lead people to seek God. We expect opportunities to strike up grace-filled conversations, and we listen attentively to each person's story. We get to know people by name and pray for them, asking God to reveal the next steps in building relationships.

There are no shortcuts to building sincere, redemptive relationships. Such relationships require genuine interest, respect, and love. So the invitational life is not about rushing into relationships or pushing for a quick response. If you have been guilty of shortcutting relationships, what commitment will you make to reset how you view relationships and allow them to be directed by prayer and God's prompting rather than by your own agenda?

TAKE ACTION

Just imagine what might happen—in your family, community, city, nation—if all followers of Jesus looked for the good in people around them, actually listened to each person's story, were sensitive to recognize and respond to the needs of people they encountered, and took advantage of every opportunity to joyfully scatter seeds of God's grace in a hurting world. That would be amazing! Why not begin now?

As you interact with people this week, guard against looking for differences or shortcomings in people. Instead, look for their positive attributes, and celebrate what is good in them wherever you see it.

Everyone matters to God, who is compassionate and generous. This week focus on being his partner in redemption, keeping your eyes alert for signs of need such as grief, brokenness, financial stress, fear, or pain. Pray about how to come alongside people and address their needs. As God is generous, be generous in praying about their needs and finding the right way to meet them.

BENEDICTION

(1 minute)

By God's redeeming power we are being built up like living stones—not silent stones, not dead stones—to become a spiritual house that honors God's mercy and displays his grace far and wide.

PART III

RELATE

Jesus was curious about people. He practiced the discipline of seeing past all the external labels. When society labeled a woman a whore, Jesus saw her as a daughter of the King. When his own disciples scowled at the tax collectors, Jesus saw broken stories and lonely people. Jesus always saw the person, not the label.

SESSION 5
IT'S JESUS OR NOTHING

People who understand that Jesus is number one naturally orient their lives around loving Christ, following Christ, and imitating Christ. A Christ-centered life is compelling. It bears the kind of fruit that people want to taste and see. It draws people in.

CONSIDER THE INVITATION

(4 minutes)

As we closed our previous session together, we turned our attention to looking for the good in the people we encounter and keeping our eyes alert to signs of need in their lives. Both of these practices are essential to developing significant relationships in which we can generously sow seeds of God's grace.

What did you discover as you intentionally looked for the good in the people you encountered rather focusing on shortcomings or differences?

In what ways did you honor and celebrate the goodness and positive attributes of other people, and how were your actions received?

It is so easy to charge through life focused exclusively on ourselves—what we need, what we do, what we want, how we feel. What was it like to step back, slow down, and intentionally seek to identify the needs of others from the viewpoint of being God's partner in redemption?

What did you see as your eyes and heart opened to the needs of the people you encountered, and how did you want to respond to them?

LET'S PRAY TOGETHER

Dear Lord, we are so grateful that you chose us and redeemed us as your beloved children. We want to faithfully obey your calling and invite everyone to experience your redeeming grace. Guide us step by step as we engage in relationships that make a difference and point the way to Jesus. Develop in us a genuine desire to get to know who people are and what is important to them. Give us a heart that cares deeply about people. Show us what is most important in our relationships with others, and help us keep what is important clearly in view. In Jesus's name we pray, amen.

VIDEO HIGHLIGHTS

(15 minutes)

Choose to take down relationship-killing barriers.

Engage in relationships at a deeper level.

VIDEO CONVERSATION

(6 minutes)

1. The scene of a man screaming through a bullhorn as a young woman wept before him is a powerful image. What were your thoughts as that scene was described to you?

When have you witnessed someone claiming to speak for God in a manner that was truly harmful to another person, and how did you respond in that situation?

In what ways did that situation influence the way you talk about God with other people?

2. What do some followers of Jesus say or do when seeking to share the good news that actually shuts down communication, stifles relationships, and creates confusion about what is most important?

3. It is easier than we think to fall into the trap of making our preferences and convictions more important than they really are—even more important than Jesus and his sacrifice to redeem us. How can we keep what is most important at the forefront, and why is it essential that we do this?

4. There are many ways to initiate conversations and encourage deeper, more significant relationships. Which ideas presented in the video were most helpful to you?

What ideas would you add for building trust and depth in your relationships with people who have not yet joined their story with God's story?

BIBLE INVESTIGATION

(15 minutes)

If we are committed to living the invitational life, we must focus on what is essential. Sharing God's story and his invitation for redemption made possible by the death and resurrection of Jesus must be our number one priority. We can't expect the world to accept God's invitation when we're all over the board promoting our personal convictions and preferences. Without Jesus at the center, we're just a collection of folks who squabble over minor points and try to push our radically varying opinions onto others.

Beyond what is essential, the way by which we share the message of Christ can make all the difference in how it is received. Sometimes *how* we share can be even more important to people than *what* we share. Let's explore how we can do a better job of developing meaningful relationships with people we encounter in life—relationships through which we can express genuine care and extend God's invitation to join in his story of redemption and restoration.

1. The Christian community in Corinth was by no means perfect. Jesus followers there faced numerous challenges and struggles that Paul addressed in his letters. To put an end to some of the conflict and arguments taking place there and other places concerning issues of preference or conviction, Paul set the record straight on what was most important. What did he say was the essential foundation of their faith? (See 1 Cor. 3:11; 15:1–6; see also Rom. 8:34; 10:9.)

Which other issues were the Corinthians squabbling about, and how were they handling some of their disagreements? (See 1 Cor. 1:10–12; 3:3; 6:1–6; 11:17–19.)

What warnings against such disagreements does the Bible provide? (See Rom. 16:17–18; 2 Tim. 2:14–16, 23–26; Titus 3:9.)

What is the result of such disagreements? (See 1 Tim. 6:3–5; 2 Tim. 2:14.)

Why do you think Paul was so concerned about these arguments and conflicts?

2. To what extent does the Christian community today face similar challenges regarding what is essential for faith?

What happens when we allow our preferences and convictions to become more important than the foundation of our faith?

In what ways does conflict regarding these lesser issues affect how people view Jesus and those who follow him and also hinder people from accepting God's gift of redemption?

3. The early Christian churches encompassed people from diverse backgrounds, religions, and cultural traditions, so it is not surprising that they experienced conflict in how they lived out their new

faith. In his letters to the churches, what did Paul emphasize about focusing on the essentials of faith in Christ while maintaining respect for the convictions and preferences of others? (See Rom. 14:1–13; Eph. 4:2–6; Col. 2:6–8.)

What can we take away from Paul's teaching that will help us keep Jesus at the center of our faith and message?

OUR LIFE RESPONSE

(4 minutes)

Jesus was a master at connecting with people in meaningful ways. He genuinely cared about all the people he encountered and wanted to get to know who they were, what they valued, and what concerned them. So he listened. He engaged in conversations. He met needs. He introduced people to God's story and invited them to join in. We also can develop genuine, caring relationships with people through which it is perfectly natural to extend an invitation to join in God's story. Consider some of the practical ways you can initiate meaningful conversations and build trust that allows relationships to go deeper.

Ask open-ended questions. The right question invites people to reveal who they really are. Jesus was a master of asking significant questions that invited deeper interaction: "Why do you call me good?" "Who do you say that I am?" "What do you want me to do for you?"

Which questions have you asked or been asked that have had a significant life impact?

Be curious. Listen intently. Think about what you would really like to know about a person and find a way to ask about it. Then ask the follow-up questions that show you really care.

In what ways do you show genuine interest and care when a person lets you in and entrusts a part of his or her story to you?

Drop your agendas. It's not about what's important to you. It's about Jesus and the person you care about. Allow yourself to be surprised. Leave room for the person to be different from what you assumed.

Our agendas and expectations for people to be or respond as we do blind us to seeing them with the eyes of God. Which agendas do you need to drop so that you can more clearly see and delight in how God's grace is working in a person's life?

Focus on potential, not differences. Differences can drive people apart, while potential encourages relationship. Focus on what a person's life could be if Jesus were at the center of it.

Which external labels that emphasize differences and put distance between people do you need to drop in order to see the potential of a redeemed life that God sees in a person?

TAKE ACTION

As you live the invitational life this week, see what happens when you focus your thoughts, prayers, and interactions on one theme: "It's Jesus or nothing!"

Think about the people with whom you have significant relationships and their need to know Jesus.

What do you really want to know about each of them?

Write down open-ended questions you might ask that could have a significant impact.

What adjustments in how you conduct your relationships do you need to make in order to orient your interactions around Jesus and his agenda rather than your pet agenda?

Write down the Christ-driven potential you see in each person. Pray specifically for it to be realized in those people's lives.

BENEDICTION

(1 minute)

As servants of Jesus our Lord, may we fix our eyes on him and through grace-filled conversations preach no message but his own—Christ died, Christ buried, Christ risen, and Christ appeared.

SESSION 6
AMBASSADORS OF HEAVEN

As ambassadors of heaven, we have the supreme honor of participating with God as he transforms lives through love. But stepping into relationships with people who do things differently, speak differently, or behave differently works only if we are centered in God's values and humbled to relinquish our judgments.

CONSIDER THE INVITATION

(4 minutes)

As we closed our previous session together, we turned our attention to how we initiate and nurture significant relationships that provide opportunities to introduce and invite people into God's story of redemption. We explored the pitfalls of focusing on our agendas rather than on God's agenda and elevating our convictions and preferences above what is most important: the redemptive work of Jesus.

How helpful was it to identify what you want to know about the people with whom you are developing significant relationships and to prepare yourself to ask open-ended questions that can help you get to know each person better?

What impact did your questions have, and which responses surprised you?

As you intentionally chose Jesus and his agenda to be the guiding focus for your interactions, what breakthrough moments occurred—perhaps in how you could foster greater trust and deeper interaction, in your understanding of who the other person is, in witnessing the compelling attraction of a life that imitates Christ, or in your hope and desire for that person to experience a redemptive relationship with God?

LET'S PRAY TOGETHER

Dear Lord, you have done so much for us that we want to obey you and share your gift of redemption and restoration with other people. But your ways are not our ways, so we need your help. We need you to teach us how to relate to others in ways that represent you and will draw people into your kingdom. Thank you that we can look to Jesus, our Lord and Savior, as our perfect example in all matters of faith and godliness. Thank you for giving the Spirit to empower us to carry the authority of Christ wherever you send us. Bless us with a rich harvest of lives transformed by your amazing love. In Jesus's name we pray, amen.

VIDEO HIGHLIGHTS

(15 minutes)

A legacy of hiding or a vibrant, adventurous life of seeking?

An ambassador: one who represents a kingdom and brings about reconciliation.

VIDEO CONVERSATION

(6 minutes)

1. Hide-and-seek is a fun game when we are kids, but it is not much fun when we grow up and hide from God when we could (and should) be seeking him. Adam and Eve hid from God because of the anxiety and shame they felt as a result of their sin. All too often we follow in their footsteps. Which parts of our story do we often try to keep hidden from our relationships with other people and with God?

What are some of the reasons we prefer to hide than to be known?

2. What did God call out to Adam and Eve, and what does he continue to call out to all his beloved children who run away and hide?

Why do you think God cares where we are? Why does he seek us out?

What did Jesus teach about seeking instead of hiding?

Why is it important for those of us who are citizens of God's kingdom to come out of hiding and seek God's kingdom continually?

3. When someone is chosen to be an ambassador, what responsibilities come with that position, and what might be the consequences if the ambassador does not represent his or her nation's interests and policies effectively?

4. Benjamin Franklin was the ambassador to France during a crucial period in America's history. Like all ambassadors, he was responsible for representing and serving the interests of his nation's head of state in a foreign land and for reconciling differences and resolving conflicts when they arose. How did Benjamin Franklin approach his responsibilities, and what was his method for preparing himself that made him effective in accomplishing his mission?

As followers of Jesus, we are sent out into the world to represent God's kingdom during a crucial period in history too. What might we learn from how Franklin conducted his mission that can help us be more effective ambassadors for God and his kingdom in our world?

BIBLE INVESTIGATION

(15 minutes)

Few of us are trained in diplomacy or experienced in the work of an ambassador, but once we accept God's gift of redemption and begin living the invitational life, we become God's ambassadors to the world!

God does not abandon us to figure out everything on our own, however. He places us exactly where he wants us to be his ambassadors. Because we represent God and his kingdom to the world, everything we do is under his authority and leadership. He sets the values we will honor and represent. His priorities have precedence over our priorities. Let's now consider what the Bible teaches us about our identity as ambassadors of heaven and how we fulfill that role.

1. In 2 Corinthians 5:17–20, Paul explained who we are in Christ and what God's redemption accomplishes in the lives of all who follow him. What did Paul say we become on behalf of God's kingdom, and what is our ministry and message?

In order to represent his King well as an ambassador, whose example did Paul say he was following? Consequently, who were the Corinthian believers to model? (See 1 Cor. 11:1.)

The work of an ambassador may be foreign to us, but God doesn't simply give us the mission and abandon us. What will he provide and do for us to ensure our success? (See Ps. 143:8; Prov. 3:5–6; Jer. 17:7–8; Phil. 4:19; 1 John 5:14–15.)

2. Paul, in Philippians 3:20, pointed out that followers of Jesus are citizens of heaven. That's where our identity belongs. That's what gives us the right to be God's ambassadors. As ambassadors of the kingdom of heaven, we must submit absolutely to the authority of Christ. Our job is to represent him, not ourselves, and to pursue his agenda, not our own. What did Jesus say about himself that must be at the root of everything we do? Why is this characteristic important in our role as ambassadors to people who are separated from God by sin? (See Matt. 11:29.)

What are some of the foundational traits that help us live a life that is worthy of our calling as Christ's ambassadors? (See Eph. 4:1–3.)

3. Perhaps the greatest obstacle to being effective ambassadors for Christ comes from the legacy of hiding that originated with Adam and Eve (see Gen. 3:6–11). What do you think Adam and Eve hoped to accomplish by hiding from God?

What do we hope to accomplish when we hide, and what impact does our hiding have on our relationships with God and other people and on our effectiveness as ambassadors of God's kingdom?

4. No matter how good we are (or think we are) at hiding from other people, can we truly hide from God? (See Jer. 16:17; 23:24; Heb. 4:13.)

5. Although we may not know how to deal with the struggles, weaknesses, sins, fears, and failures that drive us into hiding, God, our creator and loving Father, does. We may fear rejection or retribution, but God desires restoration and a deep, life-giving connection with us. How does God deal with what we want to hide, and what hope does this give us to live the invitational life? (See Pss. 25:4–10; 51:1–3, 7–13.)

6. What, then, is the solution to hiding from God? (See Deut. 4:29; Pss. 14:2; 105:4; Matt. 6:33.)

OUR LIFE RESPONSE

(4 minutes)

When Benjamin Franklin went to France in 1776 as the first US ambassador, he was a highly esteemed man. But he did not carry out his responsibilities as an arrogant know-it-all. He humbly immersed himself in the culture. He learned the language, got to know people and what they valued, and built relationships; and the people came to love him. What kind of ambassador of God's kingdom do you want to be?

What do you think humility looks like to the people with whom you are developing redemptive relationships?

How well do you know the values of the people with whom you are engaged in meaningful relationships, and in what nonthreatening ways might you learn more about what is important to them?

What might you do to learn more about the culture of the people with whom you are developing relationships? For example, what activities of interest to them might you be willing to try, such as joining them in eating a kind of food you have never had, attending a musical or sporting event in which they participate, or going to a museum or festival that showcases their interests or background?

As important as it is to learn the practices that make a good ambassador, far more important is facing the truth about our faith story. It won't end well if we are hiding rather than seeking.

When we choose to hide in our relationships with others, we keep things light and superficial, we sabotage, or we simply run away. This is not the invitational life. When we choose to hide in our relationship with God, our trust in him vanishes, other things become more important, our faith is pushed into the background, our love is diminished, and the invitational life is silenced.

When Jesus invites us to seek God's kingdom first, the language implies that seeking is an action that never ceases. We will have moments when our willingness to seek is stalled by fear, but God is always searching for us, calling out to us, inviting us to step back into sight. The choice is ours.

What is your commitment? Will you choose to seek or to hide?

TAKE ACTION

As you live your life this week, will you hide or seek?

Which parts of your story do you tend to keep tucked away in the shadows where you hope no one else will see them?

Will you bring those parts of your story out into the open to seek God's restoration and trust the Spirit to guide you into an incredible experience with God?

When we bring the parts of our story we'd love to hide out into the open, we instill courage in the hearts of others to seek rather than to hide. Who do you know who is hiding, and how might you reach out to that person and encourage him or her to step out into the open and seek God?

Which difficult parts of your story would you be willing to share with another person?

BENEDICTION

(1 minute)

Glory be to God, who through Christ is reconciling the world to himself, not counting our sins against us but entrusting to us his message of reconciliation to all people.

PART IV

RISK

A life based on the gospel of safety is sure to be a long and boring one. Life happens in the mess; character is built during struggle. We get knocked down only to discover the strength we have to rise again. All throughout the New Testament, we see people compelled by love and grace to risk it all and proclaim with their one and only life, "Not on my watch."

SESSION 7
RISK IT ALL TO LOVE

To be a disciple of Jesus means more than just loving people who are similar or socially acceptable. Jesus's disciples will love without exception, without qualification, and without question. Jesus's disciples love enough to risk it all—to dive headfirst into the pain in order to restore life to those who desperately need help.

CONSIDER THE INVITATION

(4 minutes)

As we ended our previous time together, we pulled back the curtain on our own faith stories. We asked ourselves whether we are hiders or seekers. We asked if we are willing to bring the hidden parts of our stories out of the shadows to face the light of God's love, mercy, redemption, and restoration.

Where did your choice—to hide or to seek—lead you this week?

If you shared a difficult part of your story with another person, what resulted? What impact do you think bringing your story to light had on the other person and on you, your relationship with God, and your outlook for what God will do in and through your life in the future?

In what way(s) has seeking God's help in dealing with the difficult parts of your story, rather than hiding them, made a difference in your efforts to go deep with Jesus and live the invitational life?

LET'S PRAY TOGETHER

Dear Lord, you are so faithful, wise, and gracious to forgive our sins and heal our wounds and brokenness. Thank you for teaching us and leading us in your ways. Sometimes it takes us so long to understand. Give us an unquenchable desire to seek you—always, no matter what. Lord Jesus, you risked it all to love us and gave everything to redeem us. Help us be willing to risk it all to love others as you have loved us. We want our lives to be aligned with your heartbeat for all of humanity. We want to live the invitational life. In Jesus's name we pray, amen.

VIDEO HIGHLIGHTS

(15 minutes)

Not on my watch!

Our neighbor is everyone.

VIDEO CONVERSATION

(6 minutes)

1. Opportunities to take the risk to reach out to another person in the love of Jesus can occur at any time and in any place—whether we are a tourist on vacation, a Samaritan traveling down an ancient road, or a pastor seeking a Wi-Fi connection in a Middle Eastern neighborhood in the middle of the night! Imagine yourself in each of the situations described in the video. Would you risk it all to reach out in love to another person—someone you didn't even know? Why or why not?

2. How high was the risk in each situation? Think about the number of people who drown trying to save others. What if the robbers came back for you? No one strikes up a conversation with armed Palestinian men in the middle of the night!

What would be some sensible reasons to play it safe and watch from the top of the cliff rather than dive in?

What do you think allows—or compels—a person to dive headfirst into such situations?

3. At first glance, when the moment of decision was made, not one of these situations showed signs of being a spiritually significant encounter. So how do we know what God wants us to do?

What are some clues that help us know when we need to get involved?

What is needed in order for us to be in the right place at the right time?

4. We tend to view redemptive encounters with people from a very narrow, short-term perspective. For example, did our encounter lead the other person to an immediate, spiritually significant decision? How might our understanding of risking it all to love change if we had a broader, long-term view?

Consider, for example, the impact of risking it all to save a woman from drowning and seeing forty to fifty people standing around just watching. What might God be doing in the lives of some of those people now? In the lives of the drowning woman's children?

How many people through the centuries may have made decisions of significant spiritual impact because of Jesus's story about the Good Samaritan?

What impact might a Palestinian soldier who meets Jesus for the first time have on his fellow soldiers, his family, and the refugee camp in which he lives?

BIBLE INVESTIGATION

(15 minutes)

Life with Christ is not supposed to be safe and comfortable. It is supposed to matter. God chooses all who follow Jesus to be his partners in advancing his great story of redemption to all people. We have the privilege of aligning our lives with his heartbeat for humanity. We get to love others and share his gift of life with them. We get to live lives that invite everyone we encounter to join in God's story.

This invitational life is not without risk. Whenever we do something that really matters, there is a price to pay. We face challenges, doubts, retaliation, failure, criticism, and more. But miracles happen when we exercise faith and follow God's lead into the hurt, chaos, and wounded relationships of a broken world.

1. Let's take a look at some risks we may face when we live lives that are wholly sold out to inviting everyone we encounter into God's story.

What adversity might we face when we reach out to those who aren't healthy, are needy, or are looked down on by the religious or social establishment? (See Matt. 9:10–13.)

How far out of our comfort zone might we have to stretch in order to truly love? (See Matt. 5:43–48; Luke 6:27–36.)

What might we suffer for upsetting the status quo? (See 1 Pet. 2:21–24.)

2. God's love compels us to dive in and risk it all—to do whatever it takes to invite everyone to God's table.

Consider the example of Jesus, who *had* to go through Samaria. He pursued a redemptive relationship that broke every cultural norm of the day. It was more than a risk; in his world it was crazy! How did Jesus's invitation begin, and what was the result? (See John 4:4–7, 39–42.)

Consider the urgent faith and the determination four friends demonstrated to find restoration for their paralyzed friend. How did their faith influence Jesus, and what impact did Jesus have on everyone there? (See Mark 2:1–12.)

3. This invitational life isn't something we live on our own or in our own strength. It would be foolish to risk it all on our own. We can dive in because God is with us every step of the way. When it comes to risking it all to love, we've got this! Read each of the following passages, and write down what God gives us so that we can live the invitational life.

Scripture passage	We've got this! God has our back. He leads and empowers us by:
2 Timothy 1:7	
Romans 8:31	
1 Corinthians 16:13	
Acts 4:27–31	
Ephesians 6:19–20	
2 Corinthians 3:7–12	

OUR LIFE RESPONSE

(4 minutes)

Every day people are calling out for help. Every choice we make in response matters. Every choice is a statement about what we believe God is like. Do we really believe it is okay for us as followers of Jesus to stand on the cliff and, in effect, watch people drown? Do we really want to proclaim that God wouldn't risk it all to rescue them? If not, we must choose wisely.

The stories featured in the video are powerful testimonies of what God can do when we are willing to risk it all. How does your heart connect with these stories, and how do they prompt you to respond?

The story of the Good Samaritan in Luke 10 was Jesus's way of answering the question, "Who is my neighbor?" How wide and deep is your picture of your neighbor? In what specific ways might God want you to push out the boundaries of who you call your neighbor to include more of his precious children?

In order to risk it all to respond, we must do two things. First, we must hear the call. We must recognize the opportunity to come alongside someone in need. Second, we must be committed to taking action no matter the risks. Which of these is most difficult for you?

What changes might you need to make in how you orient your daily life and activities so that you recognize the opportunities and hear God's whisper?

When it is time to take action, what causes you to hesitate or stops you in your tracks? Might it be a lack of total commitment? A lack of love? Fear, doubt, or inadequacy? What might you do to more fully align your heart and life with the heart of God?

TAKE ACTION

How eager are you to live the invitational life this week? Are you willing to dive in and see what God will do in and through you? Let's hope so! As disciples of Jesus, we are to love without exception, without qualification, and without question.

Identify a new neighbor—someone you might not have wanted to consider as your neighbor in the past—for whom you can risk it all to love. Think of ways you could reach out to that person.

Consider what may be hindering your ability to hear God's voice of guidance or to see the needs of people who desperately need God's redemption and restoration. Ask for God's forgiveness and help in learning to hear his voice more clearly and to see the needs he sees.

What may encumber your ability or willingness to dive in and risk it all to offer God's redemption and restoration?

BENEDICTION

(1 minute)

In the power of God, go forth and risk it all to love people who are in desperate need of his redemption and restoration. Keep listening for his voice. Set aside all fear. Make the bold choices that reveal what you believe about God.

SESSION 8
YOUR INVITATIONAL LIFE

An invitational life is a beautiful life. It is a life filled with deep connection to the heart of God, a life that knows what love and grace feel like. It is a life that promises a front-row seat to seeing God at work in the lives of people you know.

CONSIDER THE INVITATION

(4 minutes)

As we closed our previous session together, we turned our attention to the people Jesus has called us to love enough to risk it all in order to invite them into God's story. We looked carefully at how aware of and responsive we are to people who desperately need an invitation to join God's story of redemption and restoration.

Who did you identify as your new neighbors, people you previously overlooked or ignored when you thought of the people God wants you to love as you love yourself?

What did you discover as you attempted to reach out to them?

In what ways is God guiding your heart to love them as he loves them?

What have you realized hinders your ability or willingness to recognize people in need? To hear God prompting you to act? To respond with all your heart and soul in extending God's invitation to join his story?

In what ways did the obstacles you allowed to get in the way of recognizing and responding to the cries of people who need God's redemption hold you back from living the invitational life?

How has receiving God's forgiveness set you free to live the invitational life fully?

LET'S PRAY TOGETHER

Dear Lord, you have given us the unsurpassed gift of redemption and restoration to a life-changing relationship with you. You have given us the privilege of living a beautiful life that invites others to share the deep heart connection we enjoy with you. Thank you for giving us a front-row seat to your story, to your great work in the lives of people. Now, Lord, as we close this series, prepare us and teach us how to live the invitational life for your glory and the growth of your kingdom. We want to be ambassadors who represent you well. In everything we do and say, we want to display who you are to a world that desperately needs you. In Jesus's name we pray, amen.

VIDEO HIGHLIGHTS

(15 minutes)

Too long at the mountain.

Turn, set your journey, and go!

VIDEO CONVERSATION

(6 minutes)

1. Imagine how surprised the Israelites must have been when, after becoming settled and comfortable at Mount Horeb, God announced that they had been there too long, that it was time for them to move on. In what areas do we also become too settled in our life of faith, and why might God want us to move on to a different place?

2. Many Jesus followers are confused or intimidated by the thought of *evangelism*. We know the story of God's redemption and want to share it, but we don't quite know how.

In what ways did the explanation of evangelism and the two approaches from which people most commonly practice evangelism—eschatology or ethics—help clarify matters for you?

Does thinking about the full story of evangelism in two ways—in terms of proclaiming the truth of the fall and God's redemption and in terms of the grace we demonstrate by addressing the brokenness in the world—make the idea of sharing your faith easier or encourage you to do it? Explain your answer.

3. The video gave several examples of people who said yes to God, even if it could have been dangerous, if they wondered if they were hearing God right, or simply if a kid showed up expecting God to do something. What impact did these stories have on you?

What difference can saying yes to living the invitational life make in another person's life?

Why must we live deep with Jesus if we want to make that kind of difference in the lives of people and for God's kingdom?

BIBLE INVESTIGATION

(15 minutes)

After the Israelites established a safe, comfortable life for themselves at the foot of Mount Horeb, God said to them, "You have stayed long enough at this mountain. Turn and set your journey, and go" (Deut. 1:6–7 NASB).

1. After telling them it was time for a change, what huge assignment—laden with risk, uncertainty, and incredible opportunity—did God give the Israelites to accomplish? (See Deut. 1:7–8.)

Why was this assignment important for Israel to accomplish? (See Exod. 19:4–8; Isa. 42:5–7.)

The Israelites could not fulfill their role as God's light to the nations if they remained stuck in their comfortable, familiar life at the mountain. In which areas of our walk with God might we linger too long and get stuck so that we are unable to accomplish the good work of redemption he has for us to do?

In what ways might God let us know we've camped in one place for too long, that it is time to set our sights on his vision of what he wants to accomplish in and through us and move on?

2. A crucial part of God's message to the Israelites at the mountain was to *turn* and set their journey and go. The idea behind the word *turn* is the same as for the word *repentance*. Repentance means to change our perspective or mind-set. It represents a complete shift of priorities, a change of view that allows us to see things differently and focus our attention in a new direction. When you camp out at the foot of the mountain, it is easy to focus only on life at the foot of the mountain. What *turn*—what crucial change of perspective—did God command Israel to make? (See Deut. 30:11–20; Josh. 24:14–18.)

3. When we choose to become intentional about living the invitational life, we need to lean in to God and his Word. What perspective do the following passages of Scripture provide that can help keep us on track as we live this exciting life?

Live: Deuteronomy 6:4–6

Show Up: Psalm 5:3

Relate: 1 Peter 2:9–12

Risk: Romans 8:18–21

OUR LIFE RESPONSE

(4 minutes)

God had a dream for the Israelites, a far bigger dream than they had for themselves. But it required them to leave the familiar, risk everything, and draw close to God in total dependence. It is no different for those of us who follow Jesus today. God has a dream for us to "leave the mountain" and go to the forgotten people in forsaken places and introduce them to God's story in a way that invites them in.

You are closer than you think to living this invitational life. It's in you. God hardwired you for this. His heart beats for all people to be redeemed and restored to relationship with him. And yours does too. It's time to turn, set your journey, and go.

Using the model we have been exploring throughout this study, make your plan. Then put it into action, living intentionally with great expectation for what God will do!

Live: Go deep with Jesus. Get swept up in your own relationship with our loving God and let the invitational life spill over to others.

My plan to live:

Show up: The Spirit wants to unleash you as an ambassador for God's kingdom. Be watchful for the opportunities that will cross your path. Listen for the prompts of the Holy Spirit. Train yourself to respond without hesitation.

My plan to show up:

Relate: Engage relentlessly with the people God places on your heart. Listen to their stories. Be interesting to people by being interested in them. Be transparent with your own life story.

My plan to relate:

Risk: Dive into the unfamiliar and risk it all to make the difference God created you to make in this world.

My plan to risk:

BENEDICTION

(1 minute)

Brothers and sisters of *This Invitational Life,* may your funeral be packed with people who are nothing like you because all were welcomed at your table. May you live a life deeply aligned with God's heartbeat for humanity, every single member of it. May you scatter seeds, looking for the good, looking for the need, relentlessly inviting others to come and see what God is doing in your life and the life of your church.

May you live the kind of wild and free Jesus life that forces people to say, "What happened here?" May you see your life as a carrier and not a barrier to helping people experience full access to God. May you remember that God's story is your story and everyone's story. May you show up with great expectation, no matter where you are. Whether you're telling it at a prison or a coffee shop, may your story—all of it—be used to point people to the way of Jesus. May you listen to the whispers of the Spirit and chase after them quickly. May you incarnate the Lord's Prayer like the first disciples did in Acts 2. May you help others dominate life!

May you outseek the seeker, keeping first things first, because in the end it's simply Jesus plus nothing. May you dive in headfirst to help those you know are drowning, willing to risk it all on the One who gave everything for you. May you risk it even when it doesn't make sense. May you extend the invitation even to the people you can't stand, the people who are nothing like you, and may you have an urgency that rises up from within and makes you fill the seats in your car, tear out roofs, and approach soldiers on the other side of the world. May you go and live this invitational life!